On the Front Lines

The U.S. Navy at War

by Melissa Abramovitz

Consultant:
Thomas J. Evelyn
Lieutenant Colonel, Aviation
U.S. Army

CAPSTONE
HIGH-INTEREST
BOOKS

an imprint of Capstone Press
Mankato, Minnesota

Capstone High-Interest Books are published by Capstone Press
151 Good Counsel Drive, P.O. Box 669, Mankato, Minnesota 56002
http://www.capstone-press.com

Library of Congress Cataloging-in-Publication Data
Abramovitz, Melissa, 1954–
    The U.S. Navy at war/by Melissa Abramovitz.
    p. cm.—(On the front lines)
    Includes bibliographical references and index.
    ISBN 0-7368-0924-4
    1. United States. Navy—Juvenile literature. 2. United States.
Navy—History—20th century—Juvenile literature. [1. United States.
Navy.] I. Title. II. Series.
VA58.4 .A28 2002
359'.00973—dc21   2001000447

Summary: Gives an overview of the U.S. Navy, its mission, members, history,
recent conflicts, and modern equipment.

Editorial Credits
Blake Hoena, editor; Karen Risch, product planning editor; Steve Christensen,
    cover designer and illustrator; Katy Kudela, photo researcher

Photo Credits
Archive Photos, 10
Defense Visual Information Center, cover, 4, 7, 8, 14, 16, 19, 20, 23, 24,
    27, 28

1 2 3 4 5 6 07 06 05 04 03 02

Table of Contents

CHAPTER 1

Learn about:

- The Navy mission

- Navy members

- Navy jobs

The USS *Nicholas* attacked the Dorrah oil platforms during the Gulf War.

The U.S. Navy

During the Gulf War (1991), the USS *Nicholas* attacked the Dorrah oil platforms. These oil drilling stations are in the Persian Gulf. Iraqi troops on the platforms were spying on U.S. forces in the area.

At night, the *Nicholas* sailed to within 1 mile (1.6 kilometers) of the platforms. Several helicopters took off from the ship's deck. The helicopter pilots flew toward the platforms and fired missiles at them. The missiles destroyed two of the platforms. The crew on the *Nicholas* then fired the ship's weapons at the other platforms. The surprised Iraqi troops did not have time to fire back.

A crewmember aboard the *Nicholas* then spoke to the Iraqi soldiers over the ship's loudspeaker. He told the Iraqi troops to raise their hands if they wanted to surrender. The ship's crew captured 23 enemy soldiers during this mission. They also captured and destroyed many Iraqi weapons.

U.S. Navy Members

The crewmembers aboard the USS *Nicholas* serve in the U.S. Navy. The Navy protects the United States by patrolling the world's oceans and seas. Navy members use warships and aircraft to perform this duty.

People volunteer to serve in the military. People who join the Navy are enlisted members or officers. Enlisted members often are called seamen. Officers direct seamen in their duties. Both men and women can serve as officers and seamen.

Navy members can serve on active duty or in the reserves. Active duty members work full time in the Navy. About 375,000 people are active members of the Navy.

Reserve members work part time in the Navy. They attend training one weekend a month and serve two full weeks each year. About 180,000 people are members of the Naval Reserves. Reserve members can be called to active duty during emergencies. These emergencies may include wars.

The Navy uses aircraft and ships to protect the United States.

SEALs are specially trained members of the Navy.

Navy Jobs

Navy members work on ships or at Navy bases. Some Navy members are stationed overseas. Navy members are stationed in places like Italy and Japan. About 50,000 Navy members are stationed overseas.

Many Navy members perform non-combat jobs. Some members build ships. Mechanics keep ships, aircraft, and weapons working properly. Instructors teach at Navy schools. Navy lawyers and judges perform legal duties. Doctors and nurses care for Navy members who are sick or wounded. Chaplains perform religious duties for Navy members.

Other Navy members have combat-related duties. Pilots fly airplanes or helicopters. They may use these aircraft to attack enemy targets. Gunner's mates load and fire weapons. Navy navigators plan ships' courses using maps, charts, computers, and radar. Radar uses radio waves to locate and guide objects.

Some Navy members receive special training for secret missions. Navy SEALs perform high-risk missions. SEALs may spy on enemy forces. They also may sneak into enemy areas to attack enemy targets.

Special Boat Units (SBUs) also perform secret missions. They often transport SEALs to their mission sites.

CHAPTER 2

Learn about:

Continental forces fought against the British during the Revolutionary War.

Navy History

In the late 1700s, the Continental Congress governed the American colonies. On October 13, 1775, its members decided to create the Continental Navy. They appointed Esek Hopkins as the Navy's commander. Hopkins commanded a large fleet of trading ships. He also had commanded a warship during the French and Indian War (1754–1763).

In 1775, the Continental forces began fighting against Great Britain. The American colonies fought to gain their freedom from British rule. This war is known as the Revolutionary War (1775–1783).

The Continental Navy

The Continental Navy used frigates and schooners. Navy members turned these small supply ships into warships by adding large sails. Large sails allowed the ships to travel faster. Navy members also mounted carriage guns on the ships. These cannons were placed on the ships' decks.

The Navy performed two important missions during the Revolutionary War. It attacked British trading ships. This action prevented British trading ships from bringing supplies to British forces in the colonies. Navy ships also sailed to Europe. These ships brought back weapons and supplies for the Continental Army.

In 1781, the Continental forces defeated the British. The colonies had gained their freedom. They then became known as the United States.

But after the war, the United States still needed a strong Navy to protect its trading ships. Pirates and British Navy ships often attacked U.S. trading ships.

Important Dates

1754—The French and Indian War begins.

1775—Continental Congress creates the Continental Navy; Esek Hopkins is placed in charge of the Navy.

1798—Congress creates the Department of the Navy.

1812—War of 1812 begins.

1861—Civil War begins; Navy develops ironclad ships.

1898—Spanish-American War begins.

1908—Congress creates the Navy Nurse Corps.

1914—World War I begins; the United States enters the war in 1917.

1939—World War II begins; the United States enters the war in 1941; the U.S. Navy uses submarines, aircraft carriers, and battleships during this war.

1950—Korean War begins.

1954—Vietnam War begins; the United States begins sending troops to Vietnam in the early 1960s.

1991—Gulf War begins.

1999—Operation Allied Force begins.

Ironclad ships were first used during the Civil War.

Modern Navy

On April 30, 1798, the U.S. Congress created the Department of the Navy. This department's mission was to protect the United States from enemy attacks by sea. The Navy also protected U.S. trading ships.

Throughout its history, the Navy's mission has remained the same. It still protects the United States and its ships from attacks by sea. But the Navy has made many changes to its ships.

During the Civil War (1861–1865), the Navy began to use ironclad ships. These ships had metal plates over their wooden hulls. The plates made the ships' bodies stronger. Ironclad ships used steam engines instead of sails to move through the water.

By World War II (1939–1945), the Navy had built many types of ships. Submarines traveled underwater. Aircraft carriers allowed airplane pilots to land and take off at sea. Battleships had large guns that could hit enemy ships and land targets.

Today, the Navy has many large, powerful ships. Some ships fire missiles that can hit targets more than 1,000 miles (1,600 kilometers) away. Thousands of Navy members serve aboard some of the largest aircraft carriers. The Navy currently has more than 300 ships in active service.

CHAPTER 3

Learn about:

- **The Gulf War**

- **Tomahawk missiles**

- **Operation Allied Force**

During the Gulf War, the Navy sent several aircraft carriers to the Persian Gulf.

Recent Conflicts

Today, the Navy usually does not have to defend the United States from enemy attacks. But the Navy has played an important part in many recent conflicts.

Gulf War

In 1990, Iraqi forces invaded the Middle East country of Kuwait. The United States and its allies wanted to help free Kuwait from Iraqi control. Allies are countries that work together.

The United States and its allies sent troops to the Middle East to help Kuwait. These troops included nearly 30,000 Navy members. On January 17, 1991, U.S. and allied forces began their attack on Iraq.

Navy in the Gulf War

The Navy sent six carrier battle groups to the Persian Gulf. These groups include aircraft carriers and supply ships. They also include frigates and destroyers. These small, fast warships protect aircraft carriers from enemy attacks.

The Navy also sent mine hunting ships to the Middle East. Iraqi forces had placed more than 1,000 mines in the Persian Gulf. These devices explode when ships touch or come near them. U.S. mine hunting ships found and destroyed more than 500 mines during the war.

The Navy performed many missions. The Navy used ships to carry supplies to U.S. and allied troops. Navy doctors and nurses aboard hospital ships cared for wounded soldiers. The Navy also used its ships to prevent Iraqi trading ships from carrying supplies to Iraqi forces.

The Navy attacked enemy targets. The Navy destroyed Iraqi ships with anti-ship missiles. The Navy launched nearly 300 Tomahawk cruise missiles at enemy land targets. Tomahawk missiles can hit targets up to 1,000 miles (1,600 kilometers) away.

Navy aircraft pilots also performed many missions during the war. Pilots patrolled the Persian Gulf in P-3C Orions and S-3 Vikings. Pilots searched for enemy submarines in SH-3H Sea King helicopters. Navy pilots attacked enemy land targets and ships in F-14 Tomcats and F/A-18 Hornets.

The Navy launches Tomahawk missiles at enemy targets.

19

Navy pilots fly F/A-18 Hornets.

Operation Allied Force

In 1999, the Serbian military forced Albanians to leave their homes in Kosovo. This region is part of Serbia in the Federal Republic of Yugoslavia. U.S. and allied leaders tried to protect the Albanians. This action is known as Operation Allied Force.

Navy commanders used new technology to plan for Operation Allied Force. They used secure e-mail and telephone equipment. This new equipment allows Navy members to communicate privately. No one outside the Navy can read or listen to these messages.

More than 6,500 Navy members took part in this operation. The Navy sent several carrier battle groups to the area. These ships sailed to the Adriatic and Mediterranean Seas.

The Navy fired more than 200 Tomahawk missiles at land targets. Tomahawk missiles destroyed Serbian government and military buildings. They also destroyed defense systems, power plants, and factories.

Navy aircraft also played an important role in this conflict. EA-6B Prowlers have special equipment that jams enemy radar. This action allowed U.S. and allied planes to fly missions without being detected by enemy radar. Pilots fired missiles at enemy targets from F-14 Tomcats and F/A-18 Hornets. Pilots carried soldiers and supplies with SH-60 Seahawk helicopters. S-3B Viking pilots spied on enemy forces.

Tomahawk Cruise Missile

- **Function:** Long range missile
- **Length:** 18 feet, 3 inches (5.6 meters)
- **Weight:** 2,900 pounds (1,300 kilograms)
- **Speed:** 550 miles (880 kilometers) per hour
- **Range:** 1,000 miles (1,600 kilometers)

The Tomahawk cruise missile is an important weapon for the U.S. Navy. The Navy launches Tomahawks from ships and submarines. The Navy uses Tomahawks to attack enemy targets on land and at sea.

Tomahawk missiles fly very fast and low to the ground. Enemy radar cannot easily detect Tomahawks because they fly low to the ground.

A missile guidance system directs Tomahawk missiles to their target. A missile guidance system uses a global positioning system (GPS). A GPS uses satellites orbiting Earth to locate objects. Tomahawks are very accurate missiles because of their missile guidance system. Tomahawk missiles hit their targets about 85 percent of the time.

The Navy is working on a new Tomahawk missile. This missile is called the Tactical Tomahawk. It will be ready for use in 2003.

CHAPTER 4

Learn about:

- Women in the Navy

- The Seawolf

- UAVs

Navy members continue to train for
new missions.

Today's Navy

Most U.S. military leaders believe that there is little threat of a major war in the near future. For this reason, the government has cut military funds. The Navy has closed some bases and reduced the number of its members.

But the Navy still must be able to defend the United States. The Navy continues to improve its training and equipment. The Navy Warfare Development Command is a special unit that plans and tests new military ideas.

The Maritime Battle Center creates training exercises for Navy members. Some training exercises teach Navy members how to react to chemical and biological weapons. Biological weapons contain germs that spread deadly diseases. Chemical weapons contain deadly poisons.

New Equipment

The Navy continues to develop new equipment to help its members perform their missions. New computers and telephone systems allow Navy members on ships, in aircraft, and at bases to communicate privately.

The Rapid Airborne Mine Clearance System is a new defense system. Navy helicopter crews use this system to locate and destroy mines in the water. This system uses laser guidance. Crewmembers direct a beam of light at a mine. They then fire a missile that follows the beam of light. The missile destroys the mine.

The Navy also is developing new missiles to attack enemy targets. The Tactical Tomahawk missile is a new guided missile. It uses a global positioning system (GPS). This system uses satellites that orbit Earth. These spacecraft can locate targets anywhere on Earth. The GPS tells the missile where the target is.

High speed anti-radiation missiles (HARM) destroy enemy radar systems. These missiles have special sensors to locate enemy radar devices.

Women in the Navy

In 1908, women officially began serving in the Navy. Congress had created the Navy Nurse Corps. But women had worked as nurses aboard Navy ships before 1908. During the War of 1812 (1812–1815), women worked as contract nurses aboard Navy ships. They also had worked in Navy hospitals. These nurses were not Navy members. But the Navy paid them to work.

In 1942, the U.S. Congress passed a law allowing women to be regular members of the Navy. Since then, women have served in almost every job in the Navy. Women now command ships. They fly Navy aircraft. But Congressional law does not allow women to serve in direct combat or on submarines. Women also are not allowed to serve with SEAL or SBU units.

Today, more than 50,000 women serve in the Navy. About 8,000 of these women are officers.

New Ships

The Navy is building new ships for future missions. One new ship is the Seawolf submarine. The Seawolf is faster than other submarines. It can travel at more than 40 miles (64 kilometers) per hour. Most other submarines can only go about 35 miles (56 kilometers) per hour.

UAVs are operated by remote control.

The Navy is designing the land attack destroyer (DD 21) to attack land targets. This warship can sail close to shore. It has an electric motor. The DD 21 also will be designed to avoid enemy radar.

Another new vehicle is the Unmanned Underwater Vehicle (UUV). Navy members operate this vehicle by remote control. This ability allows the Navy to spy on enemy forces without putting its members in danger. The Navy also uses UUVs to hunt for mines.

New Aircraft

Navy members use unmanned aerial vehicles (UAVs) to spy on enemy forces. These planes are operated by remote control. UAVs have a video camera that sends pictures back to the people operating them. These pictures help Navy members learn about enemy forces.

Navy leaders hope that UAVs can be designed for combat use. The Navy then will use UAVs to drop bombs on enemy targets.

The Navy continues to protect the United States by sea. It will continue to be a strong military force with new equipment and special training for its members.

Words to Know

aircraft carrier (AIR-kraft KA-ree-ur)—a ship with a flight deck where aircraft can take off and land

allies (AL-eyes)—people, groups, or countries that work together for a common cause

enlisted member (en-LIST-id MEM-bur)—a member of the Navy who is not an officer; enlisted members also are called seamen.

mine (MINE)—a device that floats in the water and explodes when a ship sails near or into it

mission (MISH-uhn)—a military task

officer (OF-uh-sur)—a military member who directs enlisted members in their duties

radar (RAY-dar)—equipment that uses radio waves to locate distant objects

satellite (SAT-uh-lite)—a spacecraft that orbits Earth

submarine (SUHB-muh-reen)—a ship that can travel underwater

To Learn More

Burgan, Michael. *U.S. Navy Special Forces: SEAL Teams.* Warfare and Weapons. Mankato, Minn.: Capstone High-Interest Books, 2000.

Gaines, Ann Graham. *The Navy in Action.* U.S. Military Branches and Careers. Berkeley Heights, N.J.: Enslow Publishers, 2001.

Green, Michael. *The United States Navy.* Serving Your Country. Mankato, Minn.: Capstone High-Interest Books, 1998.

Useful Addresses

Naval Historical Center
805 Kidder Breese SE
Washington Navy Yard
Washington, DC 20374-5060

U.S. Navy Office of Information
805 Third Avenue
9th Floor
New York, NY 10022-7513

Internet Sites

All Hands–Magazine of the U.S. Navy
http://www.chinfo.navy.mil/navpalib/allhands/
ah-top.html

**Department of the Navy–Naval
Historical Center**
http://www.history.navy.mil

The United States Navy
http://www.navy.mil

Index